YOU

ARE

NOT

ALONE

YOU ARE NOT ALONE

A compilation of words to bring light to even the
darkest of days.

RAWINIA

This book is dedicated to those who are searching.

I pray for the day you see what it is I see.

I pray for the day you fall into his arms.

First published in 2021 by Rawinia Judson

© Rawinia Judson
The moral rights of the author have been asserted.
This book is a SpiritCast Network of Books

Author: Judson, Rawinia
Title: You Are Not Alone
ISBN: 9798551915546

Editor-in-chief: Cherise Lily Nana

Cover Design: Sarah Rose Graphic Design

Disclaimer:

The material in this publication is of the nature of general comment only, and does not represent professional advice. It is not intended to provide specific guidance for particular circumstances and it should not be relied on as the basis for any decision to take action or not take action on any matter which it covers. Readers should obtain professional advice where appropriate, before making any such decision. To the maximum extent permitted by law, the author and publisher disclaim all responsibility and liability to any person, arising directly or indirectly from any person taking or not taking action based on the information in this publication.

CONTENTS

A NOTE FROM RAWINIA

If you understood the storms I've had to ride and the demons I've had to fight to get this book out into the world, you'd understand the importance of this creation.

I've spent countless battles inside my mind asking myself why I'm publishing this book.

The truth is, to begin with, it was for self-serving purposes. It was for my ego. I wanted to be recognised, I wanted to be a writer, an author, like all the greats. All the people I've looked up to at different points in my life — Brené Brown, Gabrielle Bernstein, Rupi Kaur, to name a few. I wanted a book, not for you, but for me. I wanted the title and the identity.

As the process of curating this book unfolded, I experienced what I can only describe as a complete change in belief system. The foundations of what I believed to be true, and what I had created my life on, literally fell away at my feet. So, what do you do when what you once believed is no longer true?

Well, you acknowledge the journey, the lessons, and how it brought you to where you are today, right now in this moment.

You acknowledge all parts of you.

For me, acknowledging the parts of me I want to run away from and want to hide from the world has not only required deep levels of courage, it has also changed my life.

If we can acknowledge not only the parts we love about ourselves, but also the parts we hide and shame, with forgiveness, compassion, and love, we can transform our lives. This book is acknowledging a version of me who struggled to see the world clearly, and even though these poems were written by a version of me that I no longer resonate with, she was — and still is — a part of me and my journey.

So, although, there are words in here which I want to edit out, delete and hide away, instead I'm leaning into the words created by this version of me, in the hopes you too can acknowledge similar versions of you.

I hope in the process of not making myself wrong, you can hold grace in your heart for your own mistakes and misgivings. I hope you can see how truly beautiful you are. Every nook, every cranny, every piece of you.

I hope you can see you are not alone, and you are loved.

Some people say the quotes they see on Instagram mean nothing without change. Some people hate them because they question their ability to feel. But to me, a quote can change my life. To me, sometimes those words are the very words I need to hear to validate how I feel, to validate my existence, to remind me I'm not alone. Yes, they might be *just words*, but they're not just words to me. They breathe meaning into my life. They remind me I'm okay, just as I am. Right now, in this moment.

INTRODUCTION

Has a poem ever changed your life?

I mean, really changed your life.

For me, poetry has been the very thing which has supported my growth and my evolution. The words of another have reminded me I am not alone, and conversely, my own words have healed me, transformed me, and have held me through some of the darkest times in my life.

For this reason, I have learnt to see the beauty in words.

To this very day, I remember reading a poem by Canadian poet, Atticus, which changed my life. I say changed my life because during this time of my life I was struggling to see the light, consumed with depression and suicidal thoughts.

Somehow the words in this poem supported me to keep going. Although things felt hopeless, they helped me to see that underneath it all, there was a glimmer of light.

'Put your hand on your heart,'
the old man said.
'Inside you, there is a power,
there are ideas,
thoughts that no one has ever thought of,

there is the strength to love,
purely and intensely,
and to have someone love you back—
there is the power to make people happy,
and to make people laugh—
it's full compliments,
and the power to change lives and futures.
Don't forget that power,
and don't ever give up on it.

— Atticus Poetry

Don't ever give up on it. These six words were enough for me to keep putting one foot in front of another. Enough to remind me to keep going. Enough to remind me, *Rawinia, you are stronger and more courageous than you think.*

And that is why poetry is not just art to me. It's magic. It's medicine. It's an alchemical process where you transmute your emotions into something meaningful. It's where you share your heart with the world, and you remind others, *me too.* I'm going through the same thing as you.

I believe it takes courage to be a poet.

With poetry, you don't only show your vulnerability, you also show your darkest parts. Ultimately, poetry is shadow work on display.

What is shadow work?

Put simply, shadow work involves you illuminating the parts you don't want to see. It may be parts of yourself you run away from, hide from, or numb. It may be the parts of you which feel too hard to feel. It's the parts of you where you feel shame, guilt, fear, anger, or sadness.

When you bring awareness to these parts of you, you shine a light on the darkness, and in the process give yourself the compassion, love and forgiveness required to be able to honour these emotions instead of continuing to repress them or react to them.

You're not just sharing art; you're sharing the parts of you you've spent your life hiding from or lying to others about.

It's here, between these pages, creating, I learnt how to shine a light on the parts of me I spent 30 years of my life running away from.

It's been two years. Two years of deep healing. Unravelling. Remembering. Unfolding. Dying. Being reborn again. Deep work which has seen me open my heart time and time again. Even on the days I most want it to close. And that is the power of poetry.

Poetry opens up my heart. It asks me to surrender. It asks me to trust. It asks me to trust I am being guided, I am being led, I am being held in every single moment and every single breath. It asks me to hand it all over to something higher than me, to God.

As you read through the pages of this book, my wish is that you feel the depth of my words, the resonance, and the remembering of the parts of you perhaps you've yet to see. My wish is that you feel solace. You feel safe. You start to trust in yourself, your path, and in something bigger than you. My wish is that you open, and you continue to open over and over again.

My wish is that you are reminded you are not alone, not now, not ever.

HOW TO USE THIS BOOK

This book is designed to be read in a way which intuitively supports *you*.

You can read it from start to finish or pick exactly what it is you need to hear.

Dog ear the pages.

Highlight your favourite bits.

Draw in the margins.

Reflect. Get curious.

Journal on the questions which are asked in these pages.

Take a photo and post it on social media.

Above all else, learn to listen to what your heart is asking of you.

Yes, the Universe is testing you right now. It's testing you on your ability to let go and detach from the outcome. It's asking you what you really want and what's your 'why'. It's testing your triggers and how you react or respond. It's testing you so much right now — it feels like the Universe is out to get you. It's one thing after another. After another. But what if all of this was for you? What if all of this was teaching you how to stay true to yourself in every aspect of your life? What if all of this was teaching you how to speak up and share your truth? What if all of this was for a reason? I know it doesn't seem like it right now, but everything has a reason. Everything happens for you, to teach you something. So, if you're feeling hurt, angry, betrayed, sad, ask yourself, what is the lesson in all of this? Maybe it's to teach you how to be you and to stop trying to be someone for others. Maybe it's to teach you how to stop worrying about the future and to focus on the present. Maybe it's to teach you how to keep going and keep trying no matter how many times you fall. Whatever it is, focus on the lesson — for the lesson is where growth lies.

CHANGE

WHAT WILL YOU CHOOSE?

Sometimes change is the catalyst between things getting better, and things getting worse. Will you stay stuck in comfort? Or will you choose change?

PART OF THE PROCESS

Baby girl, this is just part of the process. Change is not easy, but sometimes it's necessary. Change can teach you so many things. It teaches you how to be agile, resilient, and strong. It teaches you how to ride the waves. At times smooth, and at times tumultuous. Change is inevitable. It is the one constant in life. It's how you deal with it that's the learning. It's how you rise, no matter how many times you fall. It's how you smile, even after all the tears. It's how you still find a multitude of things to be grateful for, no matter how much it feels uncomfortable. Yes, change can be scary, but it can also be beautiful if you let it. So please stop resisting it and embrace it. Let it in. Let it be and enjoy the ride.

NOTE TO SELF: IT'S UP TO YOU

Sometimes you have to hit rock bottom to want to change. I know because I've been there. I know because it wasn't until my world was crumbling down around me that I realised I had the power to change. Only I had the power to choose something different. Because it's true when they say the definition of insanity is doing the same thing and expecting a different result. Maybe you've tried *everything*, and things still aren't changing. You've got to try something new.

HARD TRUTH

Sometimes it's you who needs to change, not the other person.

Sometimes you need to change how you see them and perceive them. It's not their words, actions or behaviours.

HARD TRUTH II

If you want something different.

You have to do something different.

Similarly, you will have to face your fears.

ENDINGS AND BEGINNINGS

I hope you know it's all going to be okay. I hope that even amongst the darkness you can see the light. That even when things feel heavy, hard, and at times, hopeless, you believe deep down there's more. That you have faith, and you have the courage to surrender and let go. That you have the faith that God is holding you. That you have faith that it won't always be this way. I hope one day you learn to see the beauty in this space. The beauty which exists in endings and beginnings. The beauty in what it means to change.

DO IT ANYWAY

I know you're scared to change. I know you're scared to do something different. You're scared about whether or not you'll fail, fall flat on your face, or if it will all work out. I know you're used to how things are, it's easy just to stay here in this space. And I hope you can find the will deep within you to do it anyway. I hope you can take a step forward towards your dream, and you slowly walk away from the life which isn't serving you and isn't supportive. You slowly start to take a step in the direction of what it is you do want. Walking away from all it is that you don't want.

COURAGE

Please give me the courage to do the things I want to do, yet I am scared to do. Please give me the courage to let go of my trauma and not use it as an identity — like the favourite coat I wear in Winter to keep out the cold, but it's ten years old, falling to pieces, and itching and irritating my skin. My body is telling me to get rid of it. It's giving me all the signs. My body screams, *no I don't want it*, yet here I am, attached to it. Attached to it because I've had it for so long. Attached to it because that's how everyone knows me. I'm the girl with depression, I'm the girl with anxiety, I'm the girl who everyone leaves. I'm attached to the suffering because it's familiar. It keeps me comfortable because it keeps me warm. It smells like the memories I cling to, to drown out the bad. But no more. It's time for a new coat.

You don't need to be perfect.

You just need to be willing to show up.

You are more courageous than you think. Courage is not some heroic act from which stories are told. No, courage comes in those moments you least expect it. Courage is saying what you think, knowing others might disagree or criticise you. Courage comes from being honest about how you feel when people ask how you are today instead of saying, *I'm good*. It comes from being honest in every way — about speaking your truth when you know the other person has a different thought or opinion. Courage comes from trying new things and being a beginner all over again. It's about putting yourself in an environment where you know you might fail, or you know might make you uncomfortable. It's about admitting when you make a mistake. It's about apologising for the mistake. Courage comes from loving again and again, even when your heart has been broken. It's about sharing your creativity with the world. It's about spending time alone, reflecting on your thoughts. It's about slowing down when it's easier to speed up. It's about being unapologetically you in a world which tells us how we should look and think.

HARD TRUTH III

Sometimes the only way out is through.

You can't run away from your emotions and avoid them forever.

Stop waiting for the right time.

Just start.

QUESTION

It takes courage to question your reality and the status quo. Courage to ask, why? Why are things the way they are? Courage to listen to the whisper in your heart which says, this does not feel right, or, I don't believe it has to be this way. Courage to question every leader or person who has walked before you, and to even question yourself. Because change doesn't happen within those who are passive. From those who are willing to sit on the sidelines and watch. No, change happens within those at the frontline willing to pave a new way. For those who are willing to be honest and true.

What's stopping you from turning
your dreams into reality?

LETTING GO

You've always liked to hold on to things with the tightest of grips. So tight your hands are left calloused and dripping with blood from how unwilling you've been to let go. You've always had the belief that if you work hard and hope for the best, it will work out. And yes, sweet girl, it will. But what if that belief was grounded in you also learning how to let go? To trust. To free yourself of the shackles you've enslaved yourself in by holding on so tight. Let go and free yourself of the pain you've endured. Let go and let it all come to you.

START A NEW CHAPTER

Darling, you need to let go of expectations. All they do is disappoint. All you're doing is setting yourself up to get hurt. Not everyone is going to live up to your expectations. Not everything is going to end up the way you imagined it. You need to let go of the stories you have created in your head. I know they're beautiful, but they're also unhealthy. It's time to write a new story and start a new chapter. Maybe the new chapter is hard to write. I know it's frustrating rewriting the same line, over and over again. Scribbling it out, editing it, deleting it, starting it again. You can't move on until the words flow off your fingertips. I know it's frustrating you, so let the anger come if you need. Anger is part of what it means to live. It's part of the human existence, it's part of the spectrum of emotions we are meant to feel as humans. Let it come, yes, but don't let it stay for too long. Don't let it eat you up and consume you. Don't let it control you and make you bitter. You deserve to be happy. Don't let it get in the way of your own happiness by staying stuck in this chapter. Take your time if you need, but don't take too long. You've got a book to write and it's waiting for you to start.

Can you let go of all the suffering and allow yourself to be present to what's around you?

IT'S TIME

It's time.

It's time to stop looking back, and time to look at the life you want to create. It's time for you to create a life you love and a life which lights you up. It's time to create a vision for you.

It's time to stop holding yourself back. Because really, you're the one who is holding yourself back. No one else. Let's be honest. It's you and no one else.

Every time you look back, you're stopping yourself from moving forward. Every time you look back, you're stopping yourself in your tracks.

Our past is important as it holds all our lessons, however it's time to look forward and create. Creation is the antidote to suffering. You need to stop drinking your own poison. It's only hurting you.

It's time to take action.

Create a plan.

Break it down into steps.

Now go and make it happen.

HOLDING ON

I'm not ready to let go,

even though I know I need to.

Because you don't want me.

What would happen if you let go of all the stories?

GATHERING

I think sometimes it can be hard for us to let go of things. Because we're taught our value is based on what we collect. So, we hoard. We hoard not just material things; we hoard people and places. Gathering as we go about life, adding to our collection. Feeling good about ourselves from all the things we have in our life, not realising sometimes we need to clear out the closet. Sometimes we need to get rid of the jacket which no longer fits, or in this case, the person, place, or environment that we keep trying on. Sometimes we need to stop gathering and trust, our value is within. It is not an external measure. It lies deep within. Trusting value is who you are. Not what you have.

TRUST

TRUST

Darling, you just need to trust. Trust in the Universe. Trust God is watching over you. I know everything is changing. I know it's different. I know it's overwhelming and I know it's not what you want, but sometimes not getting what you want can be exactly what you need. *You just need to trust.* With every door that closes, another one opens. It's time to have the courage to walk through the door that's waiting for you with two feet in. It's time to look ahead. I know you're leaving a lot behind. It doesn't mean it wasn't important. But by stepping through the door, you are taking responsibility for your happiness and your life. *You're looking after you.* So please trust and believe, God will always provide you with everything you need — and sometimes we need the storms to learn to be strong. Remember, every storm has an ending, and every ending has a new beginning.

It's time for something new.

What would happen if you took a giant leap of faith?

You threw it all in, and instead of thinking about the outcome, you said, *fuck it,* and went all in. What's the worst that could happen?

I know, I know. There are a few not so good things that could happen. But it's not the end of the world, right? And, if it doesn't work out, then it's another lesson learnt. It's another experience of resilience. And instead of asking yourself, what if it doesn't work out, what would happen if you ask yourself, what happens if it does work out?

MIRACLES

I think we're all a little lost, and oftentimes it's these seasons of feeling lost in which the Universe is asking us to trust and have faith more than ever.

What are the things that bring you joy?
What are the moments where you feel most alive, and who are you with?

Create the space to reflect on these things and make time for the things which make you smile and make you feel good.

Learn to tune in to your body and your reactions. How do you feel? What is your gut telling you?

Please know it's okay to feel lost and not have it all figured out. Practise patience and surround yourself with those who inspire you and bring out your most authentic self.

Trust, it is in this space where miracles occur.

What if you trusted yourself fully?

What if you trusted that you knew all along. That the answer you were searching for was right there, inside of you. If only you slowed down and listened. If only you trusted yourself, and God.

What if you knew you couldn't get it wrong?

What would you do?

TRUST THE SEASON YOU ARE IN

Please trust the season you are in. Please trust that right now you're navigating Winter and the person you're comparing yourself to, they're in their Summer. Please trust and know, right now you're being asked to rest and recharge, right now you're being asked to turn inward. It's time to nurture yourself. Feed yourself. Tuck yourself away. It's time to give more deeply to you. I know it may not feel like you are doing much or you're achieving anything. I know it may seem as though you're behind or you've taken two steps back, but please remember, every season has an ending and every cycle a new beginning. Please trust the timing of life. Of your Winter and their Summer. Trust you are exactly where you are meant to be right now in this moment.

One day you will wake up and say, *I created this life.*

One day you will see, all of this was meant for a reason.

You will see the beauty in the trials and the tribulations.

You will see everything is working out exactly how it's meant to, even though right now it might not feel that way.

I know everything feels heavy and clouded.
I know you feel broken, even though you are not.
I know you feel like your heart is missing from your body.
I know you feel like you must do it all alone.

Please trust me when I say everything you deeply wish for is coming.

It is closer than you think.
If you can lean in and trust.
Even though it makes no sense right now.

Start by putting one foot in front of another.
Every day.

Let your heart lead you.
Listen.

The truth is, it's really simple. Yet we overcomplicate things. We miss the point. We spend so much time searching, outside of us, around us, yet the answer lies here with us. Right here in this moment. With ourselves, with the person standing across from us. With God. It lies in love. It lies in unlocking our hearts. Cracking our hearts wide open, again and again. Until we are overflowing with love. Until we are no longer led by fear, but rather we are led by the fullness that exists within love itself.

DIRECTION

EVERYTHING IS A CHOICE

You get to choose.

You get to choose in every moment.
Whether you go right or you go left.
If you say yes or say no.

The path you take.
It's your choice.

Do you keep walking forwards?
Do you go backwards?
Do you stay where you are right now?

What are you choosing?
What life are you living?
What do you dream of?

What choice will you make differently?

You don't have to know all the answers.

You just need to take the next step.

WANDERING

It's okay if you feel lost.
It's okay if you don't know where it is you're going.

Just trust.
Surrender.
Release the need to figure it all out.
Put one foot in front of the other.

Breathe.

You're not lost. You're just wandering.

LOST

And there is a sadness in her eyes,
the kind which hurts.

For she's tired.
She's lost.

Herself.
Her path.

She's wandering,
but not in the right direction.

And the truth is, most of the time I do not know. I do not know what tomorrow will bring, or what will become of you and me. I do not know where my next step will lead, or if it's down the right path. All I know is that I trust. I trust that even though the path might not be the one I think I need; it's the one God is leading me on. I trust that although I don't know, the breadcrumbs I can see along the way are all I need to keep going, keeping trusting that even in those moments when I get caught up in the stories, the conditioning, and the world around me, I am exactly where I need to be. And I trust.

Now is the time to start looking ahead.

It is the time to stop looking back at all the things you've allowed to affect you.

It's time to be here now.

It's time to allow the present moment to inform you, instead of the past.

It's time for you to hold the vision of the future you desire and to take action from that place.

To take one step at a time.

To do one thing a day which will bring you closer to what it is you do want.

It's time to stop focusing on the things you don't want.

The relationship you don't want.
The job you don't want.
The circumstance you don't want.

It's time to focus on what you do want. Hold that vision in your mind's eye and walk towards it.

Keep walking towards it.
Keep focusing on it.

Know it will arrive.

NOTE TO SELF: IT'S OKAY TO TAKE A STEP BACK

It's okay to take a step back. Some people believe it means you're going backwards, but what if it meant you were really pausing, observing what is, or re-routing? Sometimes we need to take a step back to see the path laid out before us. To take a breath and ask ourselves, is this *really* what I want?

CLARITY

It's okay to not know what you're doing. It's okay to not feel like things are clear right now. Not everyone has their life figured out, and there is no timeline for success. I know people in their 40s who still don't know what they want to do. I know people who are on their second, third and fourth careers. I know people who are only just figuring out the things they love and what they want to do in their 30s. It's okay. You don't have to dance with everyone. You can dance to the beat of your own drum if you want. Listen — now is the time to go out and have fun. Now is the time to try new things. Go to different classes, studios, or gyms. Book a random flight to Hawaii if it serves you. Go to a personal development workshop alone. Try new things, for it's in those experiences where you might discover that one thing. A moment of inspiration, a feeling of flow, some clarity. And until then, keep doing you and hold on to hope. It's all okay.

SOME SEASONS ARE BRIGHTER

Just know.

Everything you are feeling right now will one day pass.

And soon, what seems so foggy, seems so dark, will become clear, bright, and boundless.

For you are a girl who is caring, compassionate and loving. You are a girl in which the Universe knows to be full of light.

So just know.

Everything will one day change.

And soon the Universe will love you a little bit brighter.

ONE DAY

Even though I know it does not make sense right now.
Trust me,
one day, it will.

One day, you will see all of this was meant for you.
One day, you will wake up stronger,
happier,
fulfilled,
and whole.

One day, you will see.

TRUE NORTH

I know things don't seem clear right now. I know you're lacking the clarity and the vision to look ahead, but what would happen if you tried? What would happen if you pushed yourself to see, despite it all feeling foggy right now? I know deep down in the depths of your heart you know what you want and what's important to you. You know in your gut what feels right and what does not. You know if what you're doing is aligned to you and who you are as a person.

Listen to those things.
For they are your True North.
Your guiding light.
Your shining star.

Sweet girl, I ask you to reach deep down into the depths of you and pull these things out. I know there's a lot of fog and noise, but darling, what's going to help you most right now is direction. You don't have to know what the destination is, after all, it's about the journey. But start small and listen to what your heart is telling you.

Listen to the signs you keep seeing every day.
Listen to the times your heart flutters for the briefest of
moments.
For in those things lie the messages, the clarity, and the vision
you need to move forward with purpose.
Create the time, take the plunge. I urge you.

What if you handed it all over to God? What if, instead of trying to control and come up with an answer, you trusted God's answer? You trusted he had a plan for you. A divine plan. What if the fogginess you felt was inviting you to trust and believe? Even though logically things might not look good on the outside, or things might not be going to plan. What if you trusted God always has a plan for you?

I think sometimes we can be led to believe we always need to know where we're headed. We need to be clear on our direction and our next step, and if we are not, something is wrong with us. But here's the thing, nothing is wrong with you. Sometimes some seasons are clear, and other seasons we feel stuck. Sometimes instead of being gifted clarity, we're gifted obscurity. Yes, I say gifted. Gifted because it's asking us to slow down and listen. Gifted because it's asking us to pay attention to something else. And so, if you're feeling like things aren't clear right now. I urge you to surrender and see the magic which lies here in this space. I invite you to slow down and see, sometimes we need to slow down to see the light. Sometimes the light is in places we're scared to look — our past, our trauma, the things we reject. Sometimes the light exists when we exhale, and we trust. We keep going forward, we keep trying when we most want to give up. Sometimes the light is not found in clear blue skies, but found in thick grey fog, and the darkest of spaces.

THE ONE

If you're searching for clarity, please keep searching. Once you've found something which fits, don't try it on and keep it. As though the first choice is the answer. You wouldn't buy the first dress you try on when searching for the perfect wedding dress, would you? Well, sometimes you might, but most of the time, you try on dress after dress. Searching for the perfect one. The one which fits every inch and every curve of you. So it highlights the beauty that you are, and the purity of you. And so, as you search for clarity, I ask you to do the same. I ask you to try on something and try on more. Try on multiple ideas, multiple belief systems, until you find *the one*. Until you find the one which brings you peace and clarity. Not the one which still leaves you questioning and the one which leaves you wondering. The one which leaves you strong in your conviction and unshakeable in your faith. The one which leaves you believing deep within, even in the struggles, the hardship and the darkest of days, I know I am clear. I am clear in who I am.

COMPASSION

ONE DAY II

One day you will look at your past without fear and judgement. One day you will share with the world the stories that shaped you and the experiences and the lessons which crafted you into the gentle, loving person you are. One day — but not today. Today you are still healing from those who used your past against you. Today you're still learning to forgive yourself for the mistakes you made when you were 23 and even more recently. You're still learning to treat yourself with the compassion you give so freely to others, yet you hold back from giving to yourself. One day the stories you share will give others hope. One day the stories you tell will remind others they are not alone, and they too can rise above the darkness. One day you will tell your story to the world and you will shine brighter than you ever have before. For that is your power, your stories. For you are a storyteller, an artist, a healer, and an inspiration. You, yes, you.

STUMBLING

If you've hurt someone, I hope one day you can forgive yourself.

I hope that instead of blaming yourself and making yourself wrong, you can practise loving-kindness. You can see that, although what you did might not have been good, nice, or kind, you made a mistake, and you move on.

You apologise and you choose to make it right. Because we are human after all. Because we cannot truly know the outcome of every action.

Some people believe if you hurt someone you know exactly what you're doing. I don't truly believe in that notion.

Some instances, yes. Other instances we're acting from the deepest corners of our pain and shadows we are unable to see.

We're unable to see until we slip up, mess up and we hurt the person we love. We're unable to see until someone reveals to us what we're lying to ourselves about or hiding from ourselves.

You see, that is why I believe in second chances, even third, even more.

We don't make a mistake and we're bad forever.

Sometimes we might change in an instant, other times it might take us losing everything to break a cycle.

So, if you've made a mistake. If you've hurt someone. I hope you can see that you're learning to walk.

You might fall down a dozen times trying, but I urge you, please keep standing up.
Please keep trying.

One day you'll walk.
One day.
You'll see.

SHAME

You made a mistake. A mistake doesn't mean you're a bad person. You know the story in your head? The one you've always had, where every mistake you've made means you're bad? Well, you're not bad.

You're human.

And at times, even the best of intentions can have consequences you can't see. What matters most in those mistakes is taking on the learning and listening. I mean really listening. Asking yourself, what is this teaching me?

Admitting to yourself, *yes, I've made a mistake*, but don't stop there. Don't beat yourself up, don't let your inner victim run around in your head.

Get up, step forward, and keep going.

LET DOWN

I am proud of you for still loving yourself amongst everything that happened last year. I know you went through a lot. You made a lot of mistakes. Shit, I know you were careless and thoughtless with so many things. You cancelled on friends, repeatedly. You didn't reply to people. You ignored people. You hid from the world. You didn't ask questions or listen as intently as you could because you were so consumed with what was going on in your head. You didn't buy presents, write cards, and send well wishes for birthdays, special occasions, or momentous events. You were so consumed by you, you forgot about everyone around you — and understandably so. You were drowning in a deep, dark lake of depression and anxiety. You were fighting to breathe, and I know there were days you wanted to give up. The days when you were made to feel like everything was your fault and there was something wrong with you. The days where no matter the progress, it still wasn't enough. The days where every time you drove home from work, you saw that power pole on the corner of the road, and you wanted to keep driving ahead instead of turning right. You let a lot of people down last year, but more than anyone else, you let yourself down trying to be everything for everyone, except you.

REDEMPTION

You are not the mistakes you made,
ten years ago,
or even the ones you made today.

You are not the bitter taste of words left from others who
speak in suffering or pain.

You are the phoenix who rises through the ashes.
The warrior who never dies.

You are the one who continues to stand,
time and time again.

To fight for her honour.

Sweet soul.

I hope one day you can forgive yourself.
For all the so-called truths you believed, which were really lies.
For your naivety and your innocence.

I hope one day you can see,
you were just doing your best.

You can see,
God has been protecting you all along.

You can see,
all of it was meant for a reason.

For you to rise.
For you to become stronger.

For you to become a stand against it all.

OUT OF HIDING

How do you come out of hiding?

You forgive yourself and own the parts of you you've been so scared to own. The dark parts you've been ashamed of for so long...

...the depression

...the anxiety

...the childhood upbringing

...the alcoholism

...the drugs

...the sexual exploration.

All the parts of you which you've kept hidden away under lock and key because you're so scared that if people knew these things about you, you wouldn't be worthy of love.

SELF-WORTH

YOU ARE EXACTLY WHERE YOU'RE MEANT TO BE

Stay in your own lane, babe. You're on your own journey. Stop looking around. Joy does not come from comparison. You can't tell me you feel good every time you beat yourself up from not doing the things everyone else is doing. It's different when it's friendly competition among friends, but when you're disappointed because the girl at the gym beat you at a workout, or your friends are getting engaged, or because the girl who's younger than you has a thriving business, it doesn't mean you aren't enough. No one has walked the path you have walked or climbed the mountains you have climbed to get here today. No one's stories and chapters look quite like yours. Your path is different to everyone else's. You just need to trust it's the path set out for you and trust what lies ahead is meant for you. Don't rush it. Enjoy it. Savour every moment. You are exactly where you are meant to be right now, and everything is perfect just as it is. Just keep going.

IT'S EASY TO COMPARE

I know it's easy to compare yourself to others. What is that
really going to do?

Will it make you happy? No.
Will it make you upset? Yes.

I know things aren't easy right now.
I know you're hurting.
I know you're not happy.
Please keep trying though.

Please remember how utterly amazing you are, even on days
like today when you don't feel that way. Please remember you
are not alone, even though right now you feel so empty.

It's important to spend time alone and to feel everything
you're feeling right now. I know you want it to go away,
and one day it will. But for now, it's important to feel it and
acknowledge it.
It's teaching you so much.

It's teaching you how to love yourself again.
It's teaching you how to learn to be happy with yourself.
It's teaching you to stop comparing yourself to others.

You're alive and you're still breathing through it all.
You've survived all of your hardest days so far. You will
survive today.

Tomorrow is a new day. It's a day to start again.
Try and stay positive and focus on the good.

You've got this girl. Yes. You do.

DESERVING

Darling, you deserve to be happy. You deserve to wake up full, bright, and boundless. You deserve a self-love so strong; no person can tear you down because you believe in yourself wholeheartedly and you know deep in your heart who you are and your character. You deserve friendships which are based on authenticity. Friends who are real and honest, no matter how much it hurts. Friends who have your back no matter the mistakes you make, or the stupid shit you do that has them shaking their heads because they told you so and they saw it coming. Friends who love you for you, even when you're sitting on the phone scrolling on the couch because you're down and upset and trying to avoid reality. Friends who love you for your strengths, your quirks, and your flaws. You deserve love. I mean real love. Not the love which looks great on social media but is different behind closed doors. You deserve love which is kind and supportive. You deserve a love which is unconditional. A love which chooses you on the good days and more so on the bad. A love which knows not everything will be easy but knows working through it will help you grow and evolve. You are worth it. You deserve it all. Yes. You really do.

MORE THAN YOU KNOW

I hope you know you are valued beyond measure.

I know sometimes it doesn't feel like it. But I see how much you give and how much you contribute with an open and full heart.

I see how much you care in the way you say things and the way you are always there for others.

Thank you for being there. Thank you for being the person who gives without expectation, and who, at times, puts others first.

Thank you for being honest in how you feel and saying it like it is, unapologetically.

Thank you for being you. You are appreciated.

More than you know.

BELIEVE IN YOU

"What do you want to do?" they asked.

"What I've always wanted to do," she said.

I've always known, yet I've always let the opinions of others influence my belief in myself.

You don't have to be perfect.

You just need to be willing to show up.

PERSPECTIVE

SHIFT IN FOCUS

What are you choosing to focus on right now?

I know there're so many things you don't want, but what are the things you do want? Whatever it is you do want, focus on that, and that alone.

Prioritise the things that make you happy, that bring you joy and that you love.

If it's the gym. Go to the gym.
If you want to have fun. Make fun a priority.
Laugh with your friends.
Turn the music up loud and dance. Sing at the top of your lungs.

Spend time with people who want the same things you do.
Spend time with people who already do the things you want to do.

Give compliments, be kind, be generous.
Treat others how they want to be treated.
Be grateful for what you have right now.

Smile and know it's all going to work out.

YOU BOTH WANT THE SAME THING

Your expectations are holding you hostage. The expectations you have on your parents, your friends, and more importantly, yourself. How can you choose to look at things differently? Perhaps, it's loving your parents for exactly who they are, knowing they did the best they could. Perhaps it's giving love to your friends instead of withholding it because you've noticed they've changed. Perhaps it's a balance of being both gentler on yourself and more disciplined. Perhaps it's shifting your perspective by putting yourself in their shoes and really feeling what they're feeling, to truly understand, you both want the same thing.

BETTER THAN YESTERDAY

Focus on the progress. Focus on how far you have come. Not on how you're feeling right now in this moment. Breathe. Breathe again. Let go. Stop focusing on the negative, the external, and the things you can't control. Babe, you can't control so many things. So, stop focusing on the things you can't change. No amount of anger, frustration or hurt is going to change the situation. Breathe, let it go and focus on where you are right now. You're better than yesterday, you're better than last year — that much you know to be true. You're growing and you're learning more and more every day. I know there are some days where this doesn't feel true, but how many better days do you have than bad? What are the good things in your life? You've got so much to be grateful for, don't allow a situation or a person to affect how happy you are right now. You're worthy of happiness. You are moving forward, even though some days you take two steps back. Remind yourself how far you've come. And remember, you are the person you are right here and now.

What are the cycles and patterns you keep repeating?

Take an honest look at yourself. Where can you take responsibility in your own life for how you show up, respond, and react? What can you do to move towards everything you could ever want? It's not about your partner, your manager, your friends, or your family. It's about you. Everything you need to move forward lies within you.

It's going to take brutal honesty.

It's going to take hard work, failure, and even pain to work through some of these things you've become so attached to doing. But how do you want to feel in six months' time, one year, or five years? Do you want to keep repeating the same things over and over again? Do you want the same outcome?

Maybe you withdraw.
Maybe you avoid things.
Maybe you let what others say about you define your worth.
Maybe you mould yourself to those around you to fit in, instead of being 100% truly and authentically you.

What will happen if you keep doing the things you have always done? It's likely you'll stay stuck.

What will happen if you work on changing those behaviours? Maybe, just maybe, you'll get what you want, or what is meant for you after all.

WHAT IF

What if you were open?

What if, instead of being stuck in your ways, your opinions, and your thoughts, you tried something new?

You took off the armour you wore and what you believe to be true for just a moment. You were open to something different. And I don't mean open as in, you need to believe every word the other person says, but open in the sense that you don't become defensive, and you don't puff up in rage.

Open to hearing another person's side of the story. Open to hearing their lived experience. Open to learning from someone different to you. Someone who hasn't walked the same path or lived the life you have lived. Someone who is the complete opposite to you.

How could you be open to asking yourself, what can I learn from this person? What could this person teach me?

What if this person had the one thing I needed to hear to shift the trajectory of my life?

What if?

I think sometimes we can be so stuck in our perspectives and the way we see the world. We're so stuck because we have to believe we're right. We're so scared of not knowing, we close ourselves off to learning something different or seeing things differently. It's because here in this perspective we're comfortable, we're right. We know. And so, to question things means we're open to being wrong. And if we're wrong, it can mean our foundations of what it means to be true can crumble away. So, we become stubborn. We become righteous. We build a shell around us to protect our ego. Instead of trusting that who we are is inherent. It's not in the belief systems we wear, or the factions we divide ourselves into. It's in who we are. What if who you were was enough? What would you do then?

What if instead of overcomplicating
things, you simplified things?

You stripped it all back.

You unravelled it all.

What if, instead of adding in more,
more things to tick off your morning routine,
more goals to achieve,
more, more, more.

You choose less.
You chose quality, over quantity.

You chose to listen to your inner knowing,
instead of distracting yourself with more.

What if you zoomed in?

You were present.

You were here.
What if you saw the beauty in less,
instead of the striving for more?

EMOTIONS

STOP RUNNING

What if instead of trying to hide from all you're feeling,
you allow yourself to feel?
I mean really feel.

Where the edges of what scare you become the new norm,
and you courageously meet them,
like a new adventure or exciting date.

Where you open yourself up to what could be,
instead of the story you're telling yourself,
what is.

You see, your sensitivity is your gift.

Your ability to feel pain so much that it hurts,
is where the light lives.

It's not in running from the shadows.

It's in facing the very thing you're scared to do,
chasing your dreams,
and stepping into the light.

DISTRACTION

Who are you choosing my love, by giving in to the distraction? The distraction of coffee, food, exercise, sleep, or social media. You see, distraction is not only wrapped in alcohol, drugs or in between the legs of others. Distraction comes from being busy, from filling the void. No matter how you choose to fill it. It's a way to escape. It's the easy way out — to run, hide, and stuff. It's easy for us to say we're being healthy because we're filling our void with so-called *healthy things* — positive affirmations, exercise, or food. But an addiction is an addiction. Call it what you will. Only when you can turn inwards and face the shadows within will you start to realise how truly beautiful you are. I see the beauty. It's time you did too.

FIRST AND FOREMOST

And it's at night when I feel most alone. It's like I'm stuck between wanting to be alone and wanting to be in the company of others. When I know going out isn't going to make me feel good but staying in reminds me I still have work to do. I still have things to heal. I still have a lot of love I need to give myself. First and foremost.

SIT WITH THEM

You know those uncomfortable emotions you're feeling?
Sit with them.

Take the time alone to go deep within yourself and ask,
where is this coming from?

The answers do not lie outside of you in some external
distraction.

Alcohol,

food,

sex,

social media,

or even exercise.

No. The answers lie within you.

Choose courage over fear and take the time to truly reflect.

YOU ARE HUMAN

Sweet girl, here's the thing about your emotions.
They are not too big, too much, or uncontrollable.

You are not crazy, or overreacting.

You are human.

The thing about your emotions is they're your compass.
And the thing is you're heading South instead of following
your True North.

You're listening to the noise of others, instead of listening to
what it is you know.

It's time for you to listen. It's time for you to lead the way.

LAYERS

What if you chose yourself?

What if you chose your dreams and made them a reality?

What if you listened to the whisper in your soul instead of the twisted tongue of those who do not embody the life it is you desire?

You get to decide. You get to decide how much you want it. How much you want to choose a new reality and how persistent you will be as you walk the path. You get to decide if you step back up, or if you give in. You get to decide and to find another way. You, not anyone else, gets to decide it all.

Here you are, asking yourself, *why is this happening to me, again?* Crying to God, *I thought I had worked through all of this, I thought I was done with this lesson.* And yet here you are again. Presented with yet another learning, another lesson, another test. And it's as though the Universe is laughing at you maniacally in the background as you curl up in bed screaming to yourself, *not again.*

You react. You're hit hard with emotions. You feel hurt. You feel triggered and you feel these feelings wash all over you, consume you, and start to eat away at you.

You want to run, you want to hide, you want to avoid it all. But you don't this time.

This time you ask yourself, *what is this here to teach me?* You ask yourself, *what is it that needs healing within me?* You ask your inner child, *what love do they need?* And instead of numbing the pain, you face your fears head on and you cry. You cry and cry. You let it all out. You feel it. You express it, and you let it all go. Piece by piece. Inch by inch. Layer by layer.

I am learning. I am learning not to rush. I am learning to slow down. I am learning to listen to the undercurrent of what's alive. I am learning not to get pulled into the emotion, or the stories I tell myself. Where instead of asking myself, *what is happening to me?* I slow down and I ask, *what is this teaching me?* I am learning the sacredness in the pause. The space between reaction and response. The space between the triggers. Where I come home to the truth of what's here. I am learning the greatest act of kindness is turning inward. I am learning once more; I am my greatest love.

INTUITION

IT NEVER LIES

What if you trusted
that feeling.

The part of your body which tells you something isn't quite
right when you meet a person,
that inner knowing.

What if this time you listened to what it is you felt?
Your intuition
Your truth.

After all,
it never lies.

She finally started to listen to her gut.

Because ignoring it and listening to logic hadn't worked for her so far.

BETTER

Your intuition is stronger than you think. How can you learn to trust it, instead of question it? How can you learn to let go of what it is you think you want, to make way for something better than you imagined?

I think it can become easy to stray and easy to wander.

We're met with so many glittery lights and promises of answers. Promises of this being the next big thing, or the magic fix. The dazzle and the hurrah.

I've been there. I've been the one being sucked in, and the one doing the sucking. I've been the one easily led astray, and the one believing, well this must be the path to walk.

Believing everything that was fed to me.

Not questioning.
Not trusting.
Myself and my inner knowing.

And so, if you're feeling pulled in to the glitz and the glamour, I want to ask you this. Is this really something which feels good for you and empowers you? Or is it something which continues to leave you searching for more?

WE'RE ALL A LITTLE LOST

I think we're all a little lost, and oftentimes it's these seasons of feeling lost in which the Universe is asking us to trust our intuition more than ever. What are the things that bring you joy? What are the moments where you feel most alive and who are you with? Create the space to reflect on those things and make time for those things that make you feel good. Learn to tune into your body and your reactions. How do you feel? What is your gut telling you? Please know it's okay to feel lost and not have it all figured out.

YOU JUST KNOW

The thing is, sometimes you don't need a reason. Sometimes you just know. Sometimes there's a feeling inside of you that says leave or says stay. Sometimes logic and fact do not feel good and the advice of others feels like a suit that does not fit. You know. Trust you know what's best.

Sweet child, I pray for the day you listen. I mean, really listen to me. Instead of ignoring all the signs and the wonders. Instead of acting out and ignoring me. Sweet child, I pray for the day you hear me, you see me, and you believe in me. All the signs I send you. The whispers I gift you. The words I speak to you. All the ways I try and wake you up from your slumber. Sweet child, I pray for the day you listen. And until then, I will continue to be here. Guiding you. Lighting the way. Until the day you do.

RESILIENCE

NOTE TO SELF: JUST KEEP GOING

Just keep going.
Just keep putting one foot in front of the other.

It doesn't really matter what direction you're heading, just keep moving.

I know some days you feel like you're wandering aimlessly, so you try and convince yourself you need to know your destination. The truth is, you don't.

Sometimes when we're so focused on our destination we miss the path that's for us. Sometimes we just need to follow the small signs along the way.

You know the ones.
The ones which seem too good to be true, or the ones which drop in your lap.

Keep following the signs.
One day you'll see exactly where you're going.

ONE DAY III

One day, the life you hope for will be yours.

You just have to believe,
and continue to put in the work.
Every single day.

One day, it will all make sense,
as to why some seasons, like now, are harder than others.

One day, you will wake up and say,
I am so grateful to be alive.

One day.
It's all coming.

YOU ARE STRONGER THAN YOU THINK

I'm proud of you for trying. I'm proud of you for getting back up, day in and day out. I know how much you want to give up. I know how much you want to hide away, to disappear, and to run to the other side of the world. I'm proud of you for getting out of bed. I'm proud of you for talking to strangers. I'm proud of you for staying on this side of the world, the side of the world which feels like it's crashing down around you. I'm proud of you for being compassionate with yourself on the days you fall back down. On the days you drown yourself with red wine. On the days you eat your feelings. On the days you can't peel the covers off you. On days where you do destructive things to numb the pain you're feeling. You're only human after all. But, what I'm most proud of is you don't let those days continue. You tell yourself no more, you tell yourself I'm worth more than this right now. You get up. You go to the gym. You eat a little bit healthier. You write, and you let it all out. You treat yourself with love.

So please don't give up. Please keep trying. You're stronger than you know.

THE TRUTH ABOUT FAILURE

It's okay to start again.

It's okay to start again as many times as you need.

It does not make you a failure.
It does not make you less worthy.

Only you know the truth of your heart.

DON'T STOP BELIEVING

You will make mistakes,
keep believing.

You won't be supported by everyone,
keep believing.

You will fuck it up,
keep believing.

You will want to give up,
keep believing.

Some days you will lose all hope,
please keep believing.

I ADMIRE YOU

I love how, no matter what, you never give up on your dreams. No matter how many times you feel broken, or you feel like you're breaking. No matter the mistakes, or the so-called failures. You keep going, and you keep believing. Even on the days where all you have to eat is Mi Goreng noodles and free black coffee from the place you're staying, or the times you've had to crash at someone's home. You keep showing up, believing in the dream you hold so dear.

Trying.
Doing.
Being.
Letting go.
Surrendering.
Trying some more.

That is what I love most about you, is your belief. It's as though your faith is unshakeable. Even when you're crying days on end asking God to help you.

Oh girl, I admire you.

THE BATTLE IS NEVER LOST

She fights the demons.
Both in her mind,
and standing in front of her.

Her every day,
a battle.

Of her will.
Of her faith.

Of something more
than this life she is currently living.

Of the belief.
Life gets to be beautiful.

BELONGING

YOU'VE GOT THIS

Remember to surround yourself with good people. The ones who lift you up. Sometimes in life you'll meet people who will want to bring you down. You'll be questioned, but not from a place of curiosity, from a place of expectation. You'll be told not to do what it is you want to do. You'll be told you are naive, dumb, stupid, and unworthy…

Just know, it comes from a dark place. Just know, it's not about you. For a good human doesn't need to bring down another. What they're doing is projecting their own insecurities from within. It never was about you; it was always about them. It's the work they need to do.

So, surround yourself with those who will lift you up and tell you to follow your dreams. Those who will help you write the plan to get there.

Surround yourself with the ones who will sit with you when you cry. Surround yourself with the ones who remind you, you've got this. Because you do.

You've got this sweet girl. One day at a time. You do.

Can you learn to be alone,

and not be lonely?

You've always felt like a bit of an outsider. Someone who didn't quite fit in. Someone who was transient, who couldn't hold down a friend for very long if she tried. You'd blame yourself and ask yourself, what's wrong with me? Why don't I have any friends? You'd spend some nights crying, feeling more alone than ever. But what you've realised over the years is that it's never been about you. Well, not in the way you thought. It's been you, yes, but that's because you've grown. You've grown and those friendships no longer serve you. They served a purpose at the time, be it a lesson or a laugh. It doesn't mean they're still not your friends, but they're not the ones who get you. You know what I mean, get you on a deeper level, because you've grown and expanded — and that's okay. It's up to you to go searching for those who do. Trust and know they're coming to you — they always do.

FILL YOUR CUP

Make time for conversations with people who are going to fill your cup.

It's those conversations about the things that matter the most. It's those conversations that are more than just a superficial, *Hi, how are you? How was your day? What have you been up to this week?*

It's more than the conversations that are about what's been going on and what's been happening in your life.

It's the kind of conversations that are inspiring and create a change within you. It's the kind of conversations whereby you hear about the experiences of others, their learning and their lessons. You can empathise, relate, and take what you need.

You might be seeking solace in a person who has been through what you have been through, or it might be you giving advice to someone. Whatever it looks like — it's more.

It's not about pleasantries. It's about realness, rawness, depth. It's about the human experience and the shit no one wants to talk about — well, no one except for you, and the others you seem to attract and manifest into your life.

Those are the people you want in your life. Those are the people you want to continue to surround yourself with.

For it's in those conversations that growth occurs and you feel full. You leave with a sense of purpose and you leave feeling inspired.

Make time for those conversations.

YOU'RE NOT EVERYONE'S CUP OF TEA

You're not everyone's cup of tea, and that's okay. I mean, some people like Earl Grey, others Green Tea, some people like Chamomile. Not everyone likes every kind of tea, and the same can be said of you. It's not something to worry about though, dear. You've known your entire life. You've always struggled to fit in because you're different to the rest, and that's okay. You've got no shortage of people who love you. You provide comfort to those who do. You're soothing, just like a Peppermint Tea, to those people whose lives you impact positively, and for others, you provide a bitter taste to the lips. It doesn't mean anything is wrong with you. It just means some people will choose you, some people will try you and move on, some people will hate you. Stick with the people who choose you, over and over again. Stick with the people who find solace in your warmth and your calm. Stop trying to force the ones who don't to stay.

WHO ARE YOU SURROUNDING YOURSELF WITH?

It's about who you surround yourself with. Are they the dreamers, and the doers?

Are they the ones who support you and lift you up when you fall over? Are they optimistic to a fault?

You know the ones I'm talking about. The ones who say, next time or give it another try. The ones who say it will all happen, you just need to trust and go out there.

The ones who say, *everything happens for a reason*, and then at the same time do everything in their power to help you find a new home, or a new job, or yourself.

You know the saying; *you are the sum of the five people you spend the most time with.*

Well, who are you spending time with?

Do they stretch you?

Do they help you grow?

What if you weren't meant to fit in? What if you weren't meant to be like everyone else, and instead were meant to accept you were different and accept who you are? What if belonging meant belonging to yourself first and foremost? Where it doesn't really matter if we truly fit in with others? But instead knowing deep within, if we belong to ourselves, we have all we need right now in this moment and every moment moving forward.

STAND UP

SPEAK UP

I am still learning to find my voice. Every time I think I've stepped forward; I take two steps back. I am still learning to distinguish between what it is I really want to say versus what it is I think I should say, to ensure that I don't offend anyone. You see, when you've been shut down, and shut up, countless times on countless occasions, speaking up induces a state of fear. What will they think of me? What will they say? What will happen if I say what I want to say? Yet, despite all the times I question the wounded part of me who still needs love and attention, I speak up. I say the thing which scares me, I speak my truth. My truth is here to be spoken and I am ready to be heard.

YOU ARE NOT FOR EVERYONE

Stand up for yourself.

Your voice. Your thoughts. Your truth.

What you have to say is important.

Don't let anyone else tell you otherwise.

You are worthy. You matter.

You are enough. More than enough.

So please be true to you. No matter what.

Yes, it might make some people uncomfortable.

Some people might not agree.

Some people might even judge you.

But remember that's on them.

What matters most is you being true to you.

Please don't be afraid to shine your light.

STAND STRONG

You are not here to bite your tongue or stay silent.

No, woman.

You are here to scream and roar,
and rage with fury.

You are here to stand strong.

Two feet planted fully on the earth beneath you.
You are here to make a stand for you and those before you,
for you and those to come.

You are here to change the course of time.

I am finding my voice...

Some days it's quiet,

other days it is loud.

I want to shout and scream,

and I feel like you can't hear me.

So, I quieten.

I soften.

I go in.

I speak for me.

Not for you.

I am finding my voice for me.

ROAR

You are not here to play small.

You are here to fucking roar.

For the world needs your voice.
It needs you to speak loud and clear,
and to shout from the rooftops.

Your vision.
Your message.
Your medicine.

You did not come here to stay silent.

No, sweet girl.

You came to sing from the very depths of your soul.

I am done with fitting in.

It's time to stand up.

I am not here to be you. I am here to be me. And so please excuse me while I turn down the noise and I mute you. I mute you from all the beliefs I'm taking on, and all the truths which work for you — but not me. And so, while I mute you, I hope you know it's nothing against you. It's not that I don't like you. It's rather that I'd rather listen to my own voice, my own truth, my own inner knowing. And so please bear with me, while I take some time out, and I take some time within. It's not you. It's me.

YOU ARE NOT
FOR EVERYONE

Sweetheart, not everyone is going to like you or love you, and it's not your responsibility to convince them otherwise. It is not your responsibility to shrink so they feel better. It is not your responsibility to apologise for your existence. The moon continues to rise despite the sun. You are not here to cater to the needs of every person. You are here to shine your light. You are here to birth a new age and way of living. You are here to shine brightly and show others the way.

STOP TRYING TO FIX ME

And it's here in this world where I feel too much.
And I want to scream *fuck off* at the top of my lungs.

I'm tired.
I'm over it.
I'm done.

I'm done with people trying to fix me or make me feel better.

I just want you to fucking listen.
I just want to say how I feel.

I don't want you to give me a solution.
I don't want to feel as though I'm not worthy,
or I'm not good enough because I'm here in this space of pain.

I'm over all the fucking solutions.
I'm fucking good at solutions.

Just give me a moment to breathe and be.

I am not for everyone and that is okay.

The truth is, I'm tired.

I'm tired of being everything to everyone.

NOTE TO SELF: YOU ARE HERE TO BE YOU

You cannot control how people perceive you.

You cannot manage people's expectations.
Only you know the truth of your intentions.
Only you know the truth of your heart.
So please stop trying to explain yourself to someone who just doesn't get you.

Please stop trying to make everyone like you.

You are not here to be liked.
You are here to be you.

And here's the thing, not everyone is going to get you. Not everyone is going to understand why you do the things you do, or why you think the things you think. Not everyone is going to see you. And here's the thing, it's not your job to convince them. And it's not your job to prove. For not everyone will see what it is you see. So, if you're feeling like you don't belong, trust me when I say, it's a good thing. It's a good thing, because who you are and the way you see the world, is exactly what the world needs. It needs you. It needs your originality. Hell, it even needs disruption. It needs those who are willing to walk into the fire, knowing what lies on the other side, might be ruins. It needs those who know, the highest path is following their heart.

The truth is, you're not here to fit in. You're here to be different, you're here to stand out. You're here to lead. And in doing so, you will learn, not everyone is for you. You will learn those who love you, and those who only love a specific version of you. You will learn how to stand on your own two feet. You will learn how to be strong. Because to lead takes courage. It takes fortitude. It takes resilience. It takes the willingness to lean in, get back up and dodge the bullets. Of those who do not agree, of those who are unable to see, of those who do not get it. But here's the thing, you're meant to be different because you're here to pave a new path. You're here to create a new way of being. You're here to do big things. Big things that only you — in your fullest, unique expression — can do.

SELF-CARE

TAKE CARE OF YOU

Beautiful, it's time to start putting yourself first. For too long now, you have put others before yourself. It's one of your best qualities, and yet at the same time, your biggest weakness. You give so much to others, you forget to give to yourself. You pour and you pour, and you pour. Until you're empty and there's nothing left. Over and over again. You see the best in others, and yet the worst in yourself. It's time to start putting yourself first and seeing the best in yourself. It's time to start believing in you, because you are important, and you are of value. It's time to start taking care of yourself.

Do the things you want to do.
Do the things that bring you joy.
Do the things that light you up.

Rest. Be spontaneous. If that's what you want to do.

Whatever it is you need, do that, and only that.
It's finally time to put yourself first.

Sometimes self-care is merely getting out of bed or having a shower. Other times it means sitting in ceremony with cacao. Sometimes it means eating a big bowl of salad. Other times it means eating pasta. Sometimes it means breathwork. Other times it means Netflix. Sometimes it means drawing, singing, playing, laughing. Other times it means crying, yelling, stomping, shaking. Self-care is not a prescription. It is an inner knowing. It is knowing deep within what it is you need right now in this moment. If your self-care looks different to mine, perfect. You know what is best for you. So, listen. Listen to your body and your inner knowing. Listen to the part of you which knows self-care is the medicine you need.

LOVE IS SAFETY

Sometimes self-care is removing yourself from the chaos. It's removing yourself from the addiction, the drama and the toxicity, and it's teaching yourself, love is safety, love is comfort, love is stability.

DOING THE HARD THING FIRST

Some days it's about getting out of my own way. It's doing the hard thing first. The thing I've been avoiding for the past two days, or the thing I've been procrastinating over the past week. It's the book I haven't finished out of fear of success, and all the places I run and hide. Where I chose ease in the current moment, over doing what it is I know I need to do. It's about no longer waiting for someone to save me. No longer being the damsel, and the princess. It's about choosing to save myself and being my own hero. No longer waiting, no longer wishing. Knowing that the path to it all, is being my own love.

DAILY PRAYER

Devotion to me is not in a morning routine, which feels like a chore, or a full moon ceremony because it's now the trend. Devotion to me is in how I choose to live and lead my life. It's in feeling the sensations and the gentle warmth of my bed as I wake in the morning. It's in the aroma of my coffee and the vibrancy and appreciation of the colours and the texture in my mouth. It's in the deep presence and conversation I have with those sitting across from me. Tuning into their emotions and responding accordingly to what is here in this moment. It is listening to my body and the wisdom she holds. Resting when she is tired. Saying no when it doesn't feel right. Choosing what I truly desire instead of what will make other people happy. It's in the sound of the insects and the birds in Spring. The glistening of the sun against the dew drops. It's in life. My life is my prayer and my daily devotion.

I refuse to force. I refuse to push and exhaust myself. To pimp myself out for the notion of hard work. I know my ability to create lies not in the forced factory farming of my life-force, but in the listening and the allowing. It lies in receptivity. So instead of pushing through and hustling, I listen. I listen to what is alive within my space and I pivot. I rest. I take a break. I do something different. Because I'm not here to do discipline. I'm here for devotion — to my heart and to the divine. Devotion to letting life lead me, and trusting, it is the plan laid out for me.

Self-care is a priority.

It's not selfish.

BOUNDARIES

STOP

Stop. Stop saying yes, just to please others. Stop saying yes because that's what you think others want. Yes, it might make them happy. But what about you? What makes you happy? Is it the pressure of being everything to everyone? Darling, you can't be everything to everyone. People are going to dislike you. People are even going to hate you. But it's your choice to focus on what matters and your choice to say yes, when really, you want to say no. What happens if you say no? People might get angry, they might even be disappointed, some might even say they feel like you've let them down. But through it all, at least you know you stood true to what you want and need — and that's what matters most. You'll know as soon as the question is asked. Does this feel right? You'll feel it in the pit of your stomach. You'll know as soon as you say, *no* — you're choosing what's best for you. You are choosing what's most important. You are choosing you. Darling you need to remember; your happiness is what's most important. If you're happy, you radiate and you shine. If you are happy then you can give so much more freely to others.

So, please stop saying yes and start saying no.
Not for anyone else but you.

I DARE YOU

Just one more hour, one more paper, one more class, you say. It's only one more thing. So, you keep pushing and you keep going. You tell yourself; *I'm not going to make excuses; I can do it all.* Everyone does, don't they? You start to feel tired, *all* the time. You take something personally. You overthink the thing your workmate said to you. You don't feel like getting up and getting out of bed. You *need* another coffee to get through the day. You just want to get away to escape it all. Now I want you to imagine this; imagine what would happen if you stopped, or said no? How do you think you'd feel? Sometimes it's not about doing it all, but rather it's about doing less with more intent. Sometimes it's about learning when to rest and taking time to look after you. Next time you think, just more thing, I dare you to say no.

WHAT ARE YOU SAYING YES TO?

When you say yes to one thing, you're immediately saying no to something else.

What are the things you're saying no to by saying yes?

We don't often think of it in that way.

When you say yes, you might be saying no to time with family, time with friends, time working on your business, or time for self-care.

What are you truly prioritising by saying yes?

What does it really mean to say yes?

REST & RECOVER

It's okay to spend the day alone. It's okay to sleep in, snooze and sleep some more. You've been keeping yourself so busy, you've forgotten to stop and reflect. You've forgotten to rest and now you're here, because you've been trying to fill up your life to help you get through everything you're feeling. It's okay, we all do it sometimes. It's the cure, they say, *just keep yourself busy and you'll get through it.* Well, I call bullshit. Today's the day to rest and recover. Today's the day to think about everything you want and everything you don't want. Today's the day to fill yourself up. It's easy to slip back into bad patterns and habits, so well done for noticing what you've been doing. Not all change is instant, and sometimes it takes time. What matters most is you could see yourself falling back into what's comfortable. Where you do things to make others happy. You've always been a people pleaser — but no more. I can see the shift. I can sense it. You're waking.

I DO NOT OWE YOU ANYTHING

I may be online, but it does not make me available.

I may have my phone with me,
but it does not mean I am required to answer your message
straight away.

I get to choose what feels right for me.
I get to prioritise my own energy and output.

I do not owe you anything because you feel entitled.

I am not a 24/7 open call centre.

DESPERATION

I can feel you scraping at the bottom of my well,
desperate to drink from me.

Your thirst.
Your longing,
for something in me I am unable to give.

For something only you can water.

I can feel the constant searching
and hunger.

I cannot give you what you think you need from me.
For what you need lies within,
You.

NOT THAT KINDA GIRL

She is not the kind of girl to respond to simple flattery.

The kind of girl who will revere a *hey, how are you*, or a *nice pics* message.

No.

She is the kind of woman who requires you to pay attention. The kind of woman who wants to be revered for it all — the depths of her soul and her naked body. Want to win her over, go deeper. Ask her about the things she loves. Tell her what you love about her. Bare your own soul. Create a connection. Disrespect her boundaries and you've lost her. Message her incessantly and she'll run a mile. Step over the line without permission or consent and she's done.

SLOW DOWN

Learn to rest.
Learn to take your time.

It's okay to slow down.
It's okay to take a day off.
It's okay to just be.

You don't have to be doing things all of the time.
Your worth is not measured in your busyness or your doing.
Your worth is not measured in your achievements.

You are worthy, just as you are.
You are worthy in the stillness and the softness.

Slow down.
You are not late.

I am done with 5am wakeups and the words, hustle and grind.
I tried that once,
multiple times even,
and I burnt out.

I got sick.

So please tell me how sickness is a measure of success?
Please tell me how stress is a marker of worth.

I mean, you wouldn't say those words specifically, but you'd
say how incredible it is you're hustling and working hard.
It's like saying congratulations for being sick.

No. I won't stand for that way of being.

I won't stand for success being something that can only be
achieved through running yourself into an early grave.

I just want a simple life.

A slow life.

Where mornings are made with sunshine, coffee, and sex.

And days are spent choosing our adventure.

NOTE TO SELF: PRACTISE PATIENCE

Time is not running out. I know you feel like you should be somewhere else right now. You feel like you should be more successful, or you should have it all figured out. But who's shoulds are you listening to, anyway? Yours? Or the worlds? What does it even mean to have life figured out? What if love, joy and happiness is not found in the constant need to be somewhere we are not? What if, instead, we slowed down and trusted the timing of life? We trusted this is what we're meant to receive right now. We trusted life isn't always about flying. Sometimes it's about waiting patiently.

I hope you know it's okay to take a break. To choose yourself. That your life won't fall apart if you call in sick and rest. Not because you're physically ill, but because your sanity needs it. Because you just need a break. You need to breathe. You need to clear the tabs in your head which are full of to-dos and never-ending lists. And you just need to be. You need to remember all the ways in which your life is not about your work, or who you help. Bur rather about how you feel, and all the ways life brings you pockets of joy. Because your life isn't meant to be full of constant stress and pressure. It's not meant to feel like you're pushing shit up hill. So if you need to slow down, let this be your permission slip. Let this be the reminder you need to hear, it's okay to just be.

I'm tired. I'm over it. Of the constant need to prove. Of the bigger and the better. Of the next. When all it does is exhaust me, and all it does is pull me out of the present and the now. I've always been one to chase my dreams, but at what expense? I refuse to chase a dream where the cost is time spent with my family and those I love. I refuse to chase a dream where the cost is my health, because I'm working late, I'm working all the damn time. I'm working. Day in, day out. No, that's not life to me. No, that's not the life I desire to build. And so while people tell you the key to success is to work hard, I say no. I say no, and dig deeper into the belief, it doesn't have to be that way. And I choose to pave my own way. Even if it means taking one step forward, and two steps back. Even if it means slower.

And I'm realising even more how complicated we make things. How we're in love with the chaos and the complexity. When peace lies in simplicity. It lies in our ability to slow down and listen to our heart and to God. Yet we're so caught up in keeping busy, what's next, or trying to fill our lives. Where we try and fill our emptiness with everything outside of us, and we're left constantly searching and wanting.

NOSTALGIA

LOST IN YOU

And I still have moments where nostalgia tastes sweet.

And look through photos of you,
the very sight reminding me of the time we drank red wine
and stayed up all night or made love in a hotel room.

We trained and laughed and ate ourselves silly.

And I saw the best in you.
And you saw the best in me.
Until one day, we did not.

And one of us ran, or one of us left, and we became
strangers once more.
And despite the days, weeks, months, or years, I look at you
and smile.
I thank God for the moments we shared.
Just you and I.

Lost in love. Lost in lust.
Lost in the intensity of it all.

ADDICTION

She loves to feel.
Sometimes a bit too much, to her detriment.

For she spends her nights dreaming of lovers past.
Nostalgia, her favourite pastime.

Musky skin,
lips stained with red wine,
and sticky bodies.

Obsessed with the skeletons in her closet,
instead of the flesh and bones standing before her.

Lost in tales of darkness and demise.

THE LOVE THAT NEVER LEAVES

And although we may not be in one another's lives.
You're still here.

You're here in the learnings and the lessons.
You're here in the changes I've made.
You're here in the healing you mirrored me.

You're here in this new version of me.

AN ODE TO THOSE I'VE LOVED

If I have loved you, I have seen the light in you. The parts of you which you do not see. Your soul. Your true essence. Not the person you show the world through your actions and words. No. I loved you for who you truly are. Not who you think you are. And that is my gift.

I don't see what I want to see — a dream of who you could be. I see who you are, underneath all the layers and the masks. For my soul has always known. She knows who you are, and she will love you unconditionally until you too see those parts of you, I see.

If I have loved you, I have never stopped. No, love is not something which can be stripped away. It lives on. Always and forever.

SOME PEOPLE NEVER TRULY LEAVE

Some people never truly leave.
Some people are etched on our hearts forever,
an imprint and memory.

One we cannot erase.

And it's the small things that remind us of them.
A song, a scent, or the way someone looks at you.

And sometimes it's these very things that keep you putting one foot in front of another. No matter if they make you laugh or cry.

It's the reminder that although some people leave, they live on.

Inside of you.

UNDERNEATH MY SKIN

And there are some people whose scent lives underneath your skin. And no matter how much you try, you can't wash it off. And the sweet musk of lovers from years past drench every inch of you.

I can't get you out of my skin.

What is it you really desire my dear? Is it really the sweet lips of lovers past and warm bodies in between the sheets? Is it really the desire to be back with him? Or is it the desire to be cracked open by God? Where you feel a deep and unconditional love so strong, it brings you to your knees. Sweet girl, please stop looking back. Stop looking back and wishing for them to love you. No love is as strong as *His*.

IDENTITY

She is becoming…

The person she's always been.

You're searching for your identity,
and you can't quite seem to grasp onto something that sticks.
You try one thing, and it falls away.

Sometimes it's because you're unsure if you're trying it for you,
or if you're trying it because your best friend likes it.

Sometimes you think you like something,
but really, you don't.
You like it only because your partner does, your family does,
or because the cool girls who get all the boys do.

And in pretending to like the things you don't really like,
you lose yourself.

You lose the very essence of you.
Who you are.

THE HOMECOMING

You are coming home.

Home to the person you have always been,
awake to the wisdom, complexity, and beauty of your soul.

No longer afraid to be seen by the world.
Home to your strength and your power.

YOU ARE EXACTLY WHERE YOU ARE MEANT TO BE II

I know you don't think it right now, but you, my dear, are incredible. More than you'll ever know. You inspire, you lead, you love, and you're so many things to so many people. Your friends find counsel in you daily. When their worlds are crashing down and they don't know what to do, you find those words, words which sing true. Words that are honest, raw and changing. You speak the truth others are scared to speak, and you lift the spirit of others when they are wandering and lost. You are the rock and the foundation for many people. More than you realise. More than you know. You're attuned and affable. Your gut and your instinct can read the world well, and you always seem to know when something is wrong. I know you're hurt but believe me when I say that this feeling, it will pass. I promise you. You're hurt because you love, and you care — too much. You are a girl who wears her heart on her sleeve, and you love unconditionally, deeply and quickly. But don't let that change you. No. Your ability to see beauty, light, and love and in others is magical. Do not let your hurt change you because the world needs more love and light, and you, beautiful, you love with a heart which is kind and caring. You are passionate, opinionated, and outspoken, yet full of grace. You are a beaming light that attracts others; so, learn to accept it and run with it. You truly have so much to offer, but your kindness is your best quality. You see the good others cannot.

So, continue to be kind and remember to smile and laugh —
for they're both beautiful in their own right. Trust me when
I say you will soon find what you are searching for, or more
accurately, what is searching for you will come to you, just
when you need it. You are destined for something beautiful
and something amazing.

You are exactly where you need to be.

HARD TRUTH III

Sometimes it's you.

Not them.

I WILL NOT BE WHO YOU WANT ME TO BE

I will not be who you want me to be.
I will not twist and contort myself for your happiness.

No, I've done that.

I've done that over and over again.
Until I've drowned.
Until I've suffocated.
Until I've lost, every piece of me that made me,
me.

I will not be who you want me to be.

I will not hide what it is I want. As though my desires are too
much, too big, too difficult.
Until I shrink.
I hide.
I dim.

No.

I will not be who you want me to be.

I will not hide my dreams, my fantasies, or my fears.
Even the parts of me that seem unlovable.
You know what I mean?
The slut.

The whore.

Whatever those words even mean?

My selfishness.

And every other part of me I've learnt to love.

Yes, love.

I will not apologise.

I will not abandon.

Myself.

For you.

I will not be who you want me to be.

I will be whoever the fuck it is.

I please.

WHAT THE WORLD NEEDS

What if who you are is exactly what the world needed? You. Imperfect and perfect. Human and divine. A masterpiece and a mess. All of it. Not just the shiny parts of you. Not just the parts the world wants to see. You know what I mean. The glitz and the glamour. You. The parts of you which still feel broken. The parts of you which you're still learning to love. The parts of you which you're still scared to show the world. What if those parts were exactly what the world needed?

HOPE

KEEP DREAMING

She often dreamed.

And she was ridiculed for being a dreamer,
yet she kept dreaming.

Knowing her dreams were the vision,
pulling her forward.

Manifesting her every desire.

I WON'T SELL MY SOUL

Some days I wish the world wasn't made up of selling your soul in order to live. Where we all lived our wildest dreams and we all thrived and flourished.

I mean, I know it's but a dream, but a girl can wish.
She can hope.
She can fantasise.

You see, the thing is, people call me a dreamer and they tell me to be realistic. They tell me to pull my head out of the clouds and that it can't be done. But the thing is, if I didn't dream, I wouldn't be here.

I wouldn't be feeling the most whole and complete I've ever felt.

HOPE IS THERE

I think if you're already wishing for hope, it is there. It is there deep within you, but it's so small, perhaps you're not yet able to see. Right now, it might be faint, right now it might be hard to see, but the fact that it's in your awareness, means it's there. It's asking you to dig deeper. It's asking you to go to the places where perhaps you're scared to go. For it's there in those places you'll find peace. It's not in the running, the avoiding or the hiding. It's in the confronting.

If there's anything that's pulling me forward, it's hope. Hope that things don't have to be this way. Hope that there's more to life than this. Hope that things change, and they do not stay the same. Hope. Belief. That just because this is how things are right now, tomorrow the sun will rise and we will be gifted a new day. Hope that one day, the light I am struggling to see will fill every ounce of my being. Hope that one day, you will come home to me.

What I'm most afraid of,

is me losing hope.

MORE

Don't ever stop dreaming.

Don't ever give up.

Keep believing.

Keep hoping.

For more.

THERE'S A WAY

Please don't give up on your dreams. I know the world will have you believe it's not the right time, it's too hard, it's not realistic. But I believe it's possible. I believe it's possible no matter how many times it doesn't work, how many times you might be re-routed, how many times you might not listen to the guidance you're being given. I believe if you can dream it, you can do it. I believe if there's a dream, there's a way. It might not arrive at a time you may think. It might not arrive exactly how you first saw it. But I trust, and I have faith. If you keep holding the vision, it will come. Do you believe it will come?

ARMOUR

GATEKEEPER

She deeply desires intimacy.
And yet, she runs.

Unwilling to sit in the discomfort of truly being seen.
As an imperfectly perfect human being,
in a world which tells her she is not enough.

And yet she is the gatekeeper of it all.
Not the world.

She is the gatekeeper of every desire and dream.
If only she was willing to let it in.

SELF-SOURCE

I know you want love.

Love wants you too.
But the love you seek in others,
is the love you need to give back to you.

LET YOUR GUARD DOWN

Albeit slowly,
she let down the walls she had built around her heart.

She peeled back the layers.
She let love in.

Slowly but surely,
she began to trust and have faith once more.

DROP YOUR SWORD

I get the need to protect yourself. You've been hurt. So, you've got your shield and sword up ready to fight, but you also want love. Love is standing there looking at you. Waiting. She's waiting for you to drop your sword and welcome her in with open arms. But you're scared she might hurt you. So, you keep your shield up and you point the sword towards her and she's standing there, hoping. Waiting. Until one day she gets tired of waiting for you to drop your armour. So, she turns around and walks away.

LET ME LOVE YOU

Sweet one, I know your heart feels heavy and hard. I know you've been hurt, time and time again, and I know how deeply you want to close. But please open. Please trust.

Please let me love you.

I can only meet you as far as you are willing to meet me. There is only so much I can give before I need to choose me. There is only so much I can give to someone who has a wall up around their heart. A wall so big it's like trying to climb a fortress. And so instead of climbing, I sit and wait. I do my best to love you. Knowing I can only love you from afar. Knowing I cannot receive love from someone who has a wall around their heart.

ANOTHER

She says she doesn't need you, but she does. It's just that she's learnt how to stand on her own two feet for so long she's gotten good at holding herself up. She's forgotten how to rest back into the arms of another and allow herself the space to breathe. And she's trying to convince herself she doesn't need anyone. But her soul feels heavy and weary. It feels tired. She needs the touch of another, and the love of another. She needs the overflowing love of someone who can see, as strong as she is, she needs love. She needs someone to relax into; she needs warmth, attention and care. She needs another.

WHAT IS LOVE?

IT'S A CHOICE

Love is not easy. It involves loving a person exactly for who they are unconditionally. It's letting go of expectations of them being the person you want them to be, or the thing they *should be*. It's letting go of control and letting go of wanting them to change and meeting them where they are right now. It's holding space for them to be exactly who they are as you encourage them to grow, only at the rate and speed they can grow, and not anytime sooner. It's knowing what your standards are, yes, but knowing your standards and your expectations are two very different things, and knowing you have the choice to love them just as they are.

NEW YOU

Sometimes love does not look like happy endings.

Sometimes it looks like difficult conversations, hard truths and relationships ending.

Sometimes what is most loving is leaving. For them, and for you.

I know right now it might not feel that way.

I know right now your heart feels heavy.

It feels like you are being torn into a thousand threads.

Right now, it feels like you are dying. Because, baby girl, you are.

The old you is dying.

She is tearing herself apart.

The old you is dying, because she was no longer serving you.

The old you is dying, because the new you is waiting.

She is waiting patiently for you to rise up.

So, she can fly again once more.

SMALL MOMENTS

Love is not big grand gestures or extravagant gifts.

Love is the way you smile and look deeply into her eyes to show her you see her.

It's in the brush of your hand on her shoulder when she's feeling down.

It's holding the door open for her and getting a glass of water when you get one for yourself.

It's in the small moments.

Lying on the couch,
wrapped tightly in one another's arms.
Drinking in their scent.

Knowing in that moment you are held,
you are safe,
and you are loved.

RECIPROCITY

Love is not a spell. It is not an unhealthy attachment cast upon another, to get what? Your needs met, and your needs only. You see, I think this world has become focused on me only, forgetting that we are in relationship. Relationship being a two-way thing. Relationship being reciprocal. And I get sometimes the pendulum swings and sometimes we are the ones being leaned on, and at other times we are the ones doing the leaning. Relationship is an undying, unwavering commitment to choose love. It's you. It's me. It's us two together, choosing one another. Day in, day out.

Love is not broken promises, and heartache.

Love is safety and the surrender of trust.

NOBODY'S PERFECT

It's okay if you slip up. I mean, it's okay if you make a mistake and then you change. I think in today's age we're so quick to give up and give in. Someone hurts you. You leave. You leave them because you deserve better. And you do. You deserve better. And at the same time, no person is perfect. No person can be everything for you. So, if someone slips up and you can't give them the grace to try again. I ask you, is it really them, or is it you? What part of you is afraid? What part of you is scared to open? Because here's the thing, sometimes what's easier is leaving. It's easier to leave, than to keep your heart open when you've been hurt. It's easier to leave than it is to look inside yourself and see where it is you need to change. It's easier to leave than to grow through conflict. Nobody's perfect. Not even you.

AN OPEN LETTER TO THE GIRLS WHO STAY WHEN THEY KNOW THEY NEED TO LEAVE

Every cell in your body knows.

It's telling you to leave. The swirl in your stomach, the lump in your throat, the tears welling behind your eyes. Knowing that what you're holding on to isn't meant to be forever. And yet, you feel confused.

You're confused because he keeps coming back, telling you he loves you, and yet his actions do not match.

He doesn't want commitment.

He doesn't want to deal with your emotions.

He cheats on you,

but you cling.

You cling to the words you're so desperate to feel.

You want to feel love, and for a fleeting moment, when he utters those words, *but I love you*, you believe he means it. Because you see the best in others. And you know he does, but he doesn't love you. No. Not in the way you deserve to be loved.

TWO FEET IN

I'm not here to live life with a half heart. I'm a fully in kind-of-girl. I'm the one who follows her dreams and her desires and who people think, *she can't be doing the right thing.* I'm the one who says I love you, after meeting you once. Who tries something, fails, tries again and then moves on. I'm the one who has an idea and gives it a go. Who goes where her heart and soul lead her, even when it doesn't make sense, even when it could hurt her. For I've lived the other kind of life. Where I woke, and the days felt grey and dark. Where I didn't want to wake. And so, while some may say I'm reckless, my heart knows. She knows the joy and the beauty that comes from being alive and truly living. Of the freedom to be. Of loving and living with her heart on her sleeve.

What if, instead of waiting, you went first? You went first, and you told the person you're into that you like them. You say, *I really want to kiss you right now* or you say, *I'm really attracted to you.* I know what you're thinking. You think, it can't be that simple, or I can't do that. I know because I was once you. I know because that's not how things are done, right? You wait. You wait for the right time. You wait for a specific number of days, you wait for a certain number of dates, you wait until they don't have a boyfriend or a girlfriend. You wait. And you keep waiting. You wish they'd tell you those same words. The words you want to hear that you don't say because you're scared, or it's not the right time, or it's inappropriate. I say, fuck that. I say, say what is on your heart. Say what you can feel so deeply in every cell in your body it keeps you awake till the early hours of the morning. Tell the person you love them, you can't stop thinking about them, that you dream about them. Show them the deepest corners of your heart. Because I think that one of the greatest losses in the world is love left unsaid. It's those people you wish you had of said something to that you regret the most. It's those people you look back on and wish you had taken a chance or had the courage. Trust me when I say, nothing breaks a heart more than the words *I love you*, left unsaid.

LISTEN TO HER

Perhaps the greatest pain is not love lost,
but love left unsaid.

It is the moments where your heart calls you,
and yet you stay.

You stay silent.
You don't speak.

It's the moments where you let logic get in the way,
instead of listening to your heart.

Your heart knows.

And so perhaps that is why it hurts so much.
You abandon her.

RIGHT NOW, IT'S YOU

It's everything about you. From the moment I saw you across the room, my body knew. Even now, it's as though my soul just knows. And to those on the outside looking in, you and I, it wouldn't make sense. Two people with a past like ours, together once more. Some would call me stupid. Yet, there is a part that knows. Trusts. Trusts that whatever is meant to be, will be. And perhaps it's with you, perhaps it's without. But all I want right now is you. And so, I lean in, I trust, and I open my heart once more.

CRASHING

Some days I wish I could explain our connection to others, but I cannot.

I cannot, because I cannot find the words to describe what it means to be fucked to oblivion and to touch heaven itself here on earth.

I cannot, because to everyone outside looking in, it would seem I am mad and in need of a mental asylum, yet I know. I know beyond all mental construct you are here for a reason. A reason no person other than us, needs to know.

We might be two planets crashing into one another, but collisions create stardust. And stardust creates life itself.

WHAT IF

I know you're scared. I know you're scared if you say what you really feel, then what? What if they don't like me back? What if they think I'm too much? What if they run in the opposite direction? I see what you're saying, and what if, *what if* meant something different. What if they felt the same way? What if they were also scared to say something? What if it all worked out? You see, sometimes the only way out is through. Sometimes we need to choose courage, take a deep breath and say how we really feel because it will bring us freedom and liberation. Not because of the outcome, but rather because we had the courage to look fear in the face and do it anyway. Because in that moment, we chose discomfort. Because in that moment, we chose us. Because the thing is, if that person runs, or if they think you're too much, then they're not the person for you. The person for you will love all of you. The person for you will say yes. So instead of waiting and wondering. Why not say how you really feel? If you don't, it's a no either way. If you do, well, who knows what might happen?

YET AGAIN

And here I am, yet again, hurting.

Asking myself, why is it I ignore so many of the things so many people run from?

Asking myself, why do I stay when people show me who they really are?

And I'll tell you why.

It's because I was once them.

I was once the person who others gave up on so easily.

I was once the person who people left,

because I was so broken and damaged.

So, I stay.

Because I see who they truly are beneath all the scars and the tears.

I see the version of them God sees.

The version people are not willing to hold in regard, and instead they believe they're the version everyone else tells them they are.

And so, that is the reason it's hard for me to leave.

REBIRTH

What is certain is that the sun will rise tomorrow, and you will
be gifted a fresh start.

A new beginning
An opportunity to start again.

For that is the beauty of tomorrows.
Of sunrises and sunsets.
A chance to die again and start once more.

A chance to create and be whoever it is you desire.
A chance to see life through a new set of eyes every time they
open.

A chance to see.
Really see.
The gift of life.
But only once you wake from the depths of your slumber.

THE ETERNAL FLAME

The eternal flame lives within you.

Some days it is but an ember in the ashes,
others it is a raging fire of destruction.

It never dies.

It lives forever,
within you.

THE PHOENIX

She was awakening.

Through the fire,
and the ashes.

She was rising.

How many times can you recreate yourself?

As many times as you like.

NO MORE

What if you could start again? What if one day you decided to wake up and decided, I'm done with this way of being and I'm done with this way of living. What if you got so tired of this way of being, you decided, no more?

I have died a million deaths,

and I will continue to do so.

REVEALING

She never truly dies.

She sheds a skin that no longer feels like it fits.

A skin which feels too tight, withered, and old.

Only to reveal the truth of her.

A deeper layer.

Another level.

A continual revealing.

Of who she is, and always was.

RE-WILD

WILDFLOWER

She is the wildflower amongst the roses,
the one with a wild heart.

The kind of heart which loves so deeply,
you feel both alive and scared,
at the same time.

THE DEPTHS OF LOVE

The thing about her is her depth.

She is deeper than the ocean,
and for some,
it can be frightening.

It's frightening to get lost in her.

Her emotions, a tidal wave or storm.

Few are willing to meet her.
Yet for those who dare,
she will show them her warmth.

She will show them what it means to feel alive.

A WOMAN WHO KNOWS

She listens to her wild heart,
the calling deep within.

Allowing her heart to lead her.
A deep surrendering in trust.

To some, she seems reckless.
To others, she seems free.

To her, she is she.

A woman who listens to the beat of her own drum.
A woman who lives her own expression.
A woman who speaks her truth.

A woman who knows, she is everything.

HOLY ANGER

She was chaos and uncontrollable.

Wildfire.
Enraged.

A wrath,
and a storm.

The death of it all.

WHAT IT MEANS TO BE A WOMAN

She has lived many chapters and many lives.

Complex,
like the Universe.
The kind of woman who takes lifetimes to read.

Each layer only part of her story.

She is the kind of woman who will confuse you,
in her very being.
Unpredictable.

Kind one day,
and then ruthless the next.
The embodiment of it all.

Unapologetic in her fullness.

For she knows her magic lies not in the comfort of her
predictability.
But in the freedom and the flow,
in her willingness to surrender to it all.

IGNITE

She will turn you on.

She will ignite something within.

Something you were unable to feel.
Something you didn't even know existed.
Until she shone her light.

Her existence alone,
the fuel to your fire.

EVER EVOLVING

And just when you think you know her,
she surprises you.

She unveils another layer.

Something new.
Something that's been hiding deep within her.
Another revelation of herself,
an excavation of her soul.

Another woman who you've yet to meet.
Another iteration.

For you cannot truly know her,
she is a woman who is ever evolving.

BEAUTY

THE UNIVERSE ITSELF

She is more than a star.

She is the whole constellation,
the entire galaxy.

Each detail as complex as the next.
Each detail a beauty to behold.

She is the sun.

A light in the darkness.

The promise of tomorrow.

THE MAGIC IS IN YOU

And the thing is,
the magic is in you.

It's not in faraway places,
or material things.

It's not in people,
or accomplishments.
Goals won or lost.

It's in the ordinary,
the mundane.

It's in the beauty,
the simplicity.

It's in learning to see.

The magic has been with you,
all along.

DIVINE BLESSING

My wish is you get to taste the nectar of your own divinity,
the sweetness of your soul.

My wish is you get to lick the edges of your own life force.

You get to fuck you.

You fall in love with every part of you.
Your softness.
Your wildness.
Your all.

My wish is you see the beauty within.
The grace of your being.
Your very existence and presence here on this earth,
a divine blessing.

HER

She can see what it is you're unable to see.

The light,
and the shadows.
The love,
and the pain.

She feels you.

She can taste the essence of your energy,
through her presence alone.

With her, you feel seen.
With her, you feel held.

You can't quite put it into words.
There's something about her.

Her
Just her.

You're drawn to her.

You are a human being.

A collection and collision of imperfect things,
that together create something beautiful.

THE BEAUTY IN YOUR SCARS

My wish is you see the beauty in your scars. You see the beauty in the way the light rolls off your hips. You see the beauty in all of you. Your smile. Your uniqueness. In you. My wish is you learn to love all of you. Where you love all parts of you so deeply, you do not wish to shape and mould yourself. Cut yourself. Inject yourself. Where you accept all of you. Where you see the beauty in the way your dimples frame your face when you smile. Where you see you. The way I see you. The way I created you. A perfect example of me. A perfect specimen. Beautiful, pure, and innocent.

ALIVE

IT IS HERE

It is in this moment where I feel most alive.

It is not in adventures in places afar.
It's here, between the sheets in a room with moss-coloured
wallpaper and wine-coloured curtains, in my old home.
It's here, listening to the hum of the traffic and the rain
dripping from the eaves.
It's here, listening to the elegance and beauty of Ludovico
Einaudi.
It's here, reading the pages of this very book.

It's here. Not elsewhere.
You need not go anywhere to feel alive.
You're already alive.
If you can see what it is I see.

PURE PRESENCE

And right now, in this moment, I feel nothing but peace.

No desires.
No demons.
Nothing but pure, unequivocal peace.

For all that has been,
and all that has yet to come.
Of the life I am living.

And I savour this moment,
knowing that just as the sun rises and falls.
So too does this moment.

THE SIMPLE THINGS

And it's the simple things I love.

The coziness of a warm bed.
The first sip of coffee.
The way the sun rises in the morning.
The smile of a stranger passing.
The feel of a new book.
The embrace of another.

Yes,
it's the simple things I love.

I AM HERE

Sweet child,
you are never alone.

Even when you feel like you are.
I am right here with you.

Holding you,
loving you
walking before you.

Leading the way.

I am here,
inside your heart.

WHAT IT MEANS TO LIVE

And somewhere along the way she forgot about pure,
unadulterated joy.

She forgot how to live.

I don't mean living in the sense of nine to five. No.
I mean living and doing what makes you feel most alive.

The experiences which touch your heart so deeply you want
to cry.

Be it the brush of the wind against your cheek,
or making love with pure presence.

You know those moments.

When you close your eyes and you dance your heart out,
because the music touches every inch of your soul,
and you swear the music was written just for you.

Those moments where you do the thing you're so scared to do.

Those are the moments.

The moments which leave you breathless and spinning.

The moments that remind you, how fucking great is this life
I'm living?

Make more time for those moments.

Make more time for the moments that leave you laughing so
hard it hurts,
or asking yourself, *is this really happening?*

Because we only get this one life.
Make sure it's one worth living.

DO YOU KNOW WHAT IT FEELS LIKE TO BE ALIVE?

Do you know what it feels like to be alive?

I mean alive and not just living.

I don't mean living from day to day. Where you wake up, eat, sleep and repeat.

I mean alive in the way that you cry multiple times a day not from grief but from the joy and the blessing of what it means to be alive.

Where the music moves you and it's as though the lyrics were written just for you.

And the drink you're sipping on tastes like nectar from the gods and it electrifies every cell in your body.

Where you're excited about what the day might bring, and you feel free.

What it means to truly live — beyond all the shoulds, the to-dos, the expectations, and the conditioning.

If not today, my wish is one day, you do.

REMEMBER ME

Sweet child, I pray for the day you see the light. Where you awaken to the truth of what is, and you see. Where you're no longer left searching or wandering and you arrive here. Home. Where you feel alive, in every moment, every breath and every prayer. Where you see the joy and love in the way you live your life. Where you realise the gift of this life is living. It's not in escaping, running away or bypassing. Of trying to be somewhere you're not. It's here. On this earth. Two feet planted firmly on the earth beneath you. Listening to the song of the birds and feeling the wind kiss your skin. It's here in the sunlight streaming on your face. Sweet child, I pray. I pray for the day you remember me, and in that moment, you arrive home, safely in my arms.

ACKNOWLEDGEMENTS

Thank you to Christine Clarkson for believing in me and encouraging me. For seeing what it is I was unable to see and for helping me to believe in myself, my writing and the gift of my words.

Thank you to my cousins, Martin and Rangitahi. Thank you for believing in me and supporting me before seeing my writing and my work. Your support seeded the courage and commitment to follow through with this book, without, I possibly would never have finished, and for that I am grateful.

My family — my dad, my brother, my Aunty Shirley, and my niece Gaia. Thank you all for being my steady foundation and my home. Through all my ups and downs. Through all my mistakes, fuck ups, and failures. Thank you for always loving me, even in the moments you want to shake me. I appreciate you. I love you. I am grateful for you.

Mum — you may not be here in this physical realm, but I am grateful for your spirit. Thank you, for gifting me with the spirit of what it means to live — to go all in, to not hold back, to live and love with my all.

My community — thank you for reading my words and finding solace in them. I write just as much for you as I do for me. This book is for you. Thank you for being a part of this journey and for being on this wild ride which is life with me.

God, Atua — thank you for gifting me with this life and for guiding me on this journey and waka. I do not know what the rest of this life will bring but I know whatever comes is part of your divine plan.

Lastly, to anyone I have ever loved — friends, partners, lovers. Thank you for teaching me, laughing with me and crying with me. Whatever our relationship looks like today, know I hold a piece of you inside my heart.

Rawinia Judson is a writer, speaker, and coach for all things connection.

Rawinia spent the better part of ten years in and out of states of depression and high-functioning anxiety. Despite this, Rawinia successfully transformed her life studying connection, emotional resilience, and spirituality. She now supports those who believe there is more to life as they currently know it.

Rawinia has become a source of deep inquiry, possibility and curiousity, helping guide others to remember who they are and live with purpose.

www.rawiniajudson.com

Printed in Great Britain
by Amazon